BOOK 2
Revised

MUSIC for PIANO

Robert Pace

WALTZ

1. First use "block" chords in the left hand, then with a down-up wrist motion, play as written. Each time you play this, notice the patterns (sequences) in the melody. Mark these.

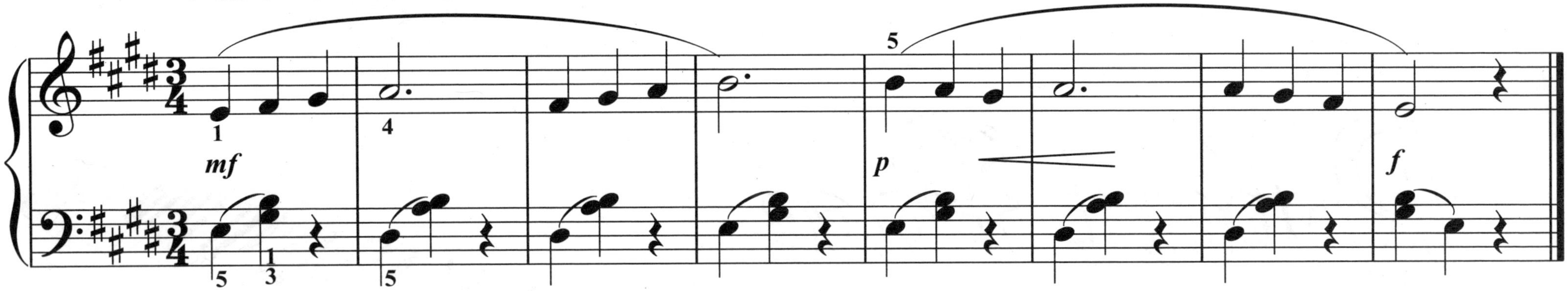

Transpose to E♭ Major, then each day try a different key.

WALTZ

(Variation)

2. Mark the passing tones (PT) then the upper and lower neighbors (UN, LN) in the melody. Each day change a few of the melody notes to create variations.

SHORT AND LIVELY

1. Play this with very firmly curved fingers. Use a "down-up" wrist motion for each note but do not move your arm. Notice how the pattern is repeated in the other hand.

STACCATO ETUDE

2. Again use a very precise wrist motion with firm fingers. Notice the contrary movement between treble and bass.

DAMPER PEDAL

Each of these signs tells us to push the damper pedal (right pedal) down, then take it up.

Ped. .... ❋

Keep your heel on the floor as you press down on the pedal with the fore-part of your foot. Be sure the pedal comes completely up as you change chords, but don't let it "thump." Also listen carefully to avoid a blur.

First play the I and V7 chords in the key of D Major as you practice pushing the pedal down and letting it up carefully.

I	V7	I	V7	
down-up	down-up	down-up	down-up	(etc.)

PEDAL ETUDE

Now play "Pedal Etude" and use pedal.

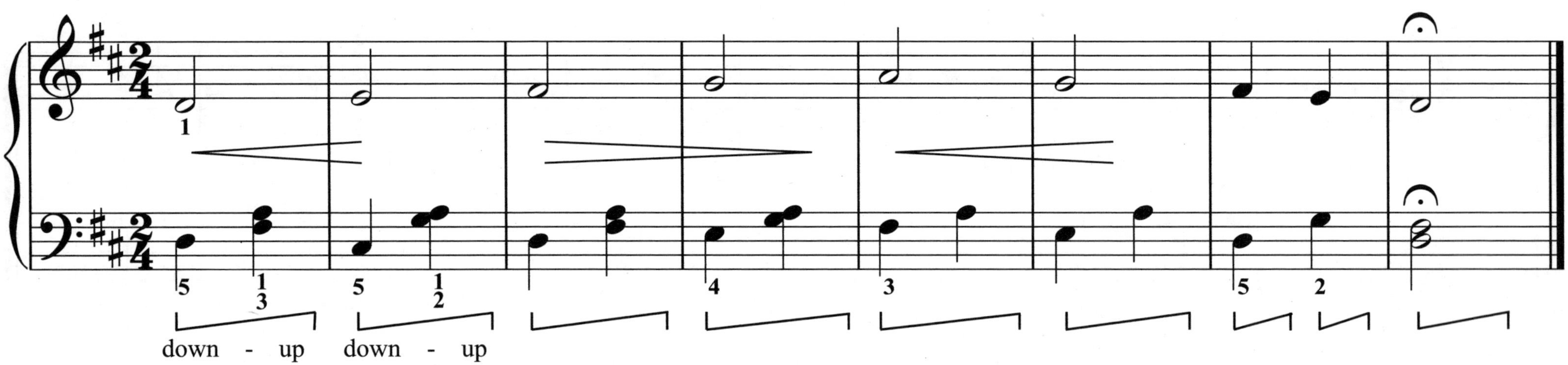

CHORD COLORS

A piece is *bi-chordal* when the chords are different in the left and right hands as in this example. Play these chords to hear the bi-chordal sounds.

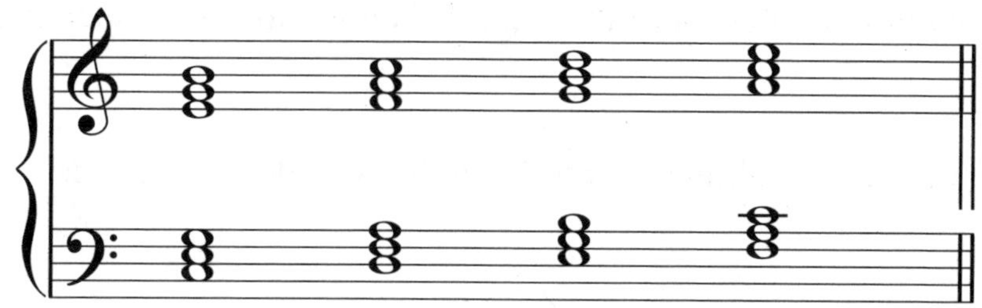

Change your pedal as marked and remember that the fermata (𝄐) means to hold the note longer.

SONG

1. Notice that only two notes of the I and V7 chord appear in each measure in the left hand.

2. Observe the pedal makings carefully so that you do not blur the melody.

DORIAN DANCE

This piece is in the Dorian mode (white notes from D to D). After playing as written, transpose it up one whole step to play in the Phrygian mode.

Pay special attention to the fingering in measures 3, 5 and 6.

FRÈRE JACQUES

(Secondo)

First play this round with these dynamics, then after a few days try other dynamics. Also switch parts with your partner.

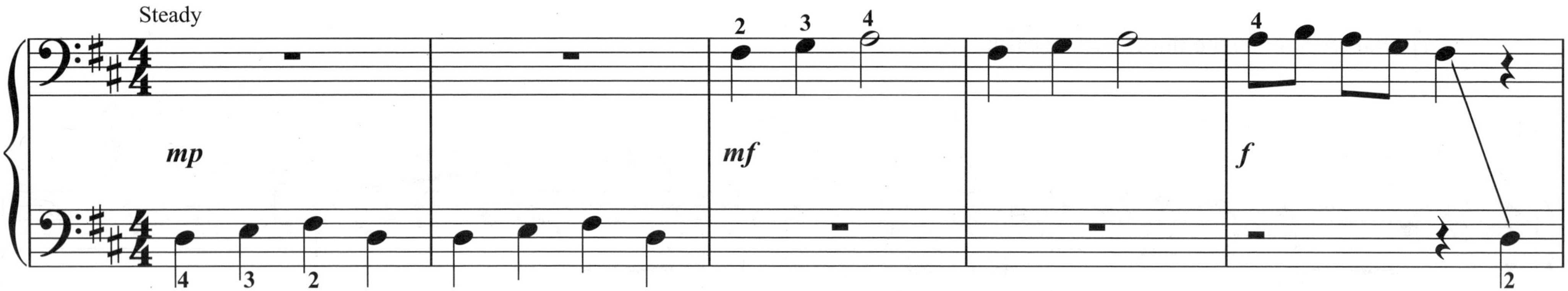

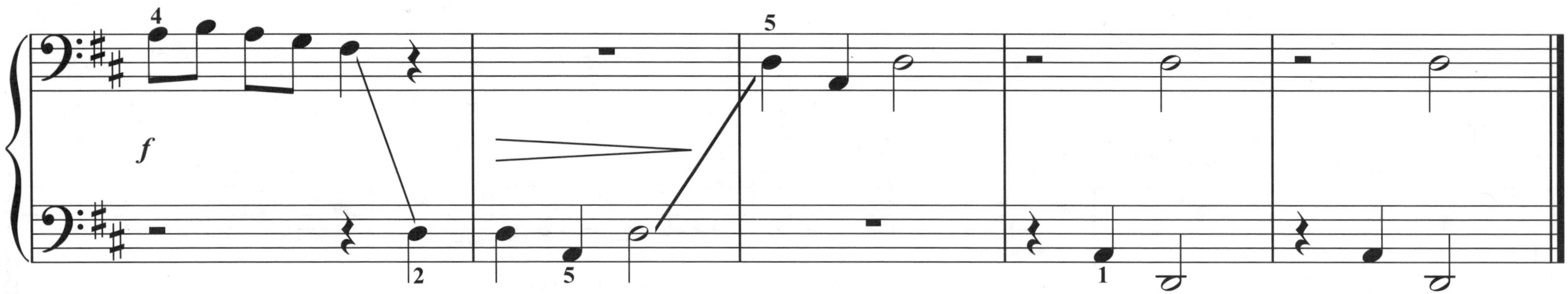

FRÈRE JACQUES

(Primo)

First play this round with these dynamics, then after a few days try other dynamics. Also switch parts with your partner.

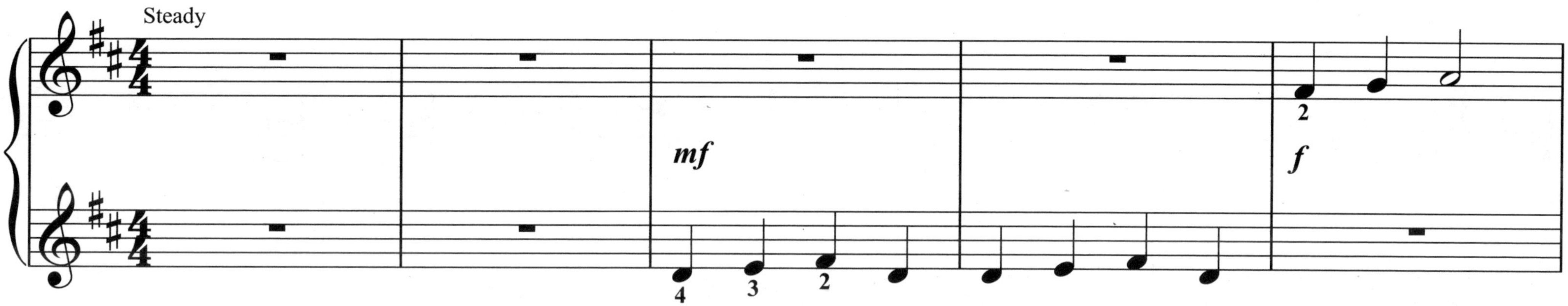

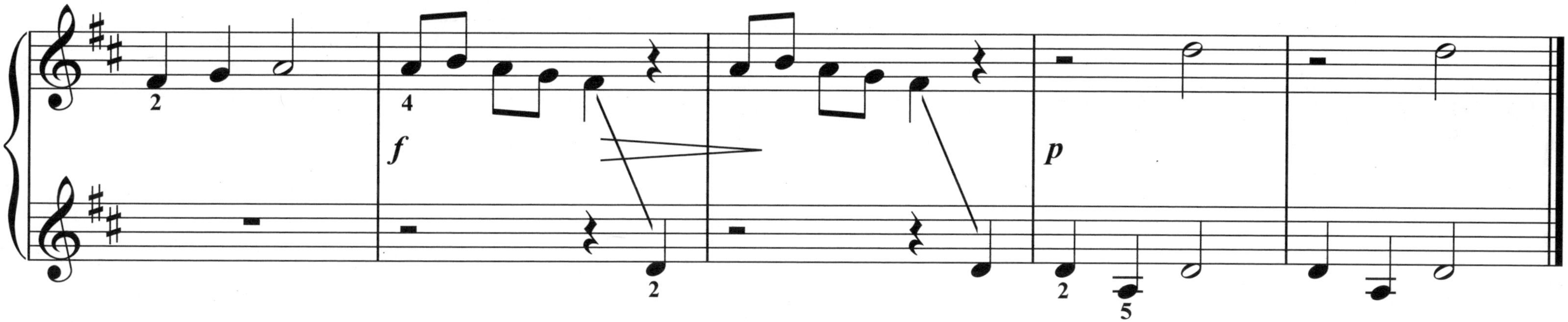

DREAMING

Notice that this piece has both $\frac{6}{4}$ and $\frac{5}{4}$ meter. Play it very quietly and use a slight stroking motion on the *portato* notes ( ).

VARIATION

This song uses the rhythm of "Mary Had a Little Lamb" but has a new melody that is harmonized by the three notes of the I chord (d f♯ a) played as an *ostinato.* First play it as written, then transpose just the left hand to C major and play it as a *bi-tonal* variation (RH-D major, LH-C major).

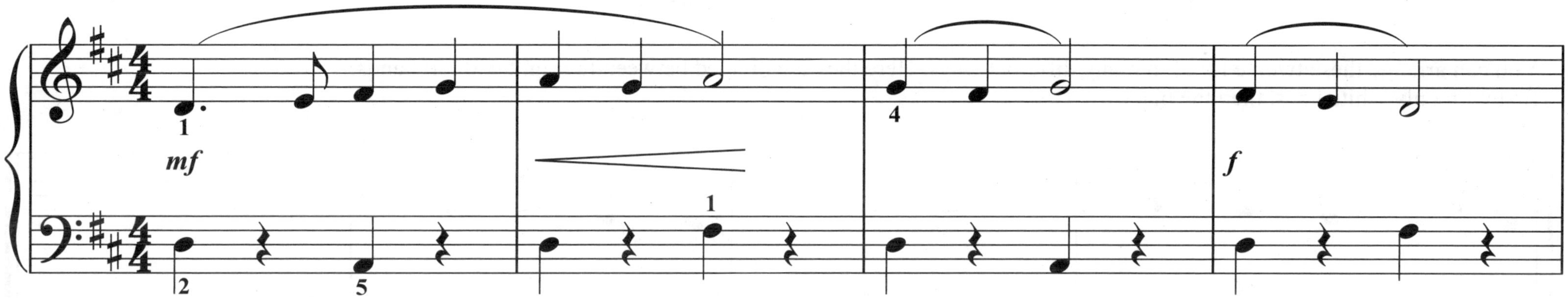

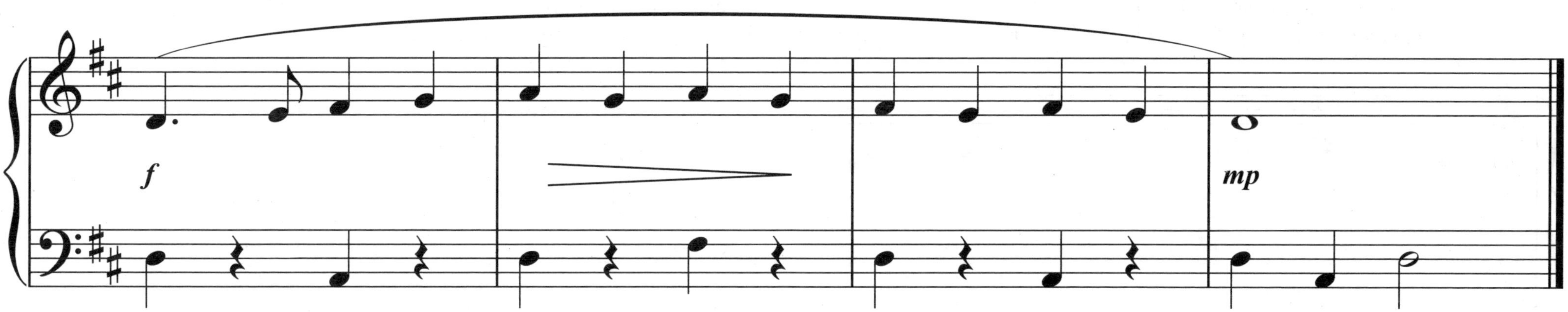

TWELVE TONES

There are twelve different tones on the piano keyboard. Play them as indicated here.

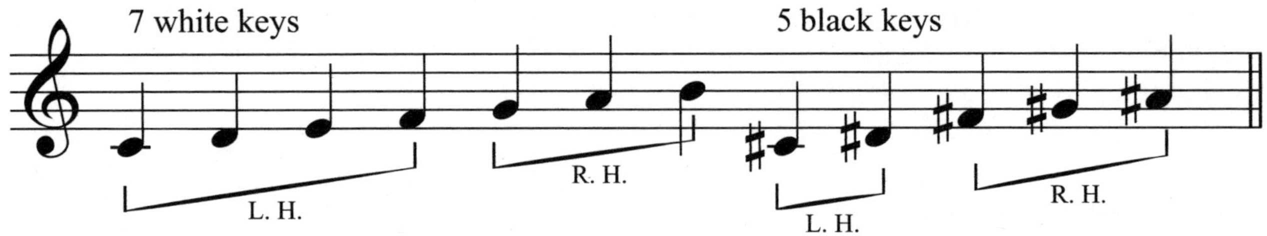

You can arrange these twelve tones in many different ways. Here they are divided between the right and left hands, first with only white keys, then the black.

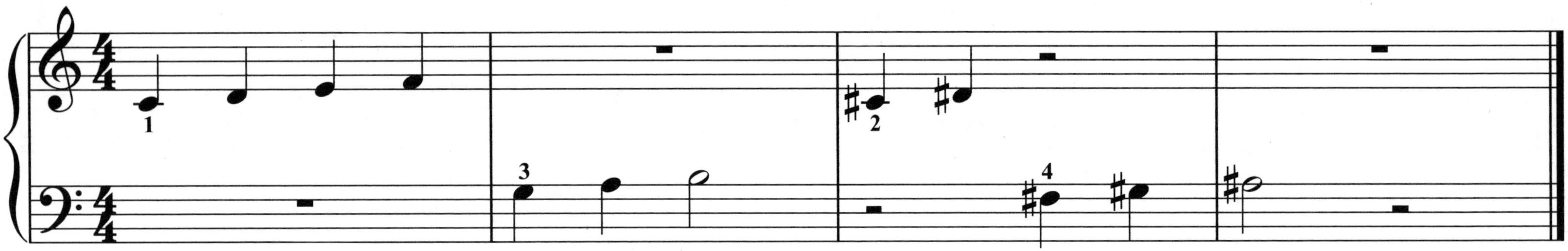

Composers can arrange these twelve tones in many different ways. Here is an example using all twelve tones before any one is repeated (called a *tone row* or *series*). The circled number refers to the order in which that tone first appeared in the row.

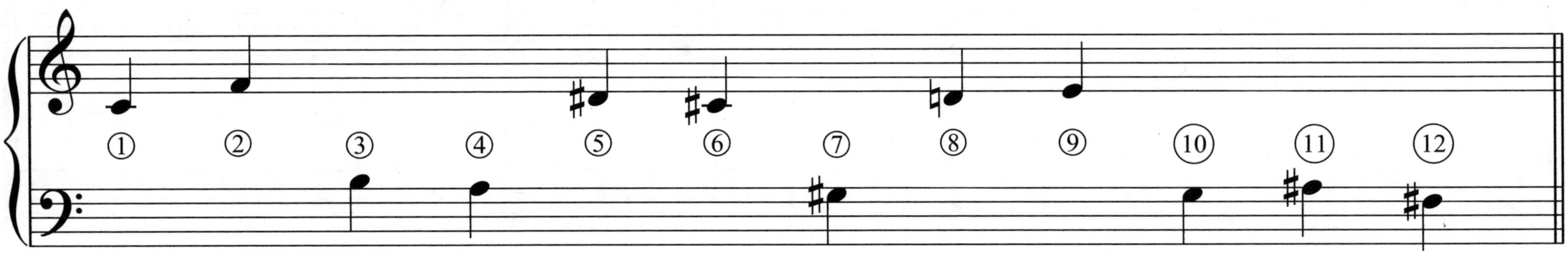

TWELVE TONE VARIANTS

1. You can give the row any meter or note values that you choose. After playing as written, change the rhythm of measures 1, 2 and 3. Remember that the circled number refers to the order in the series.

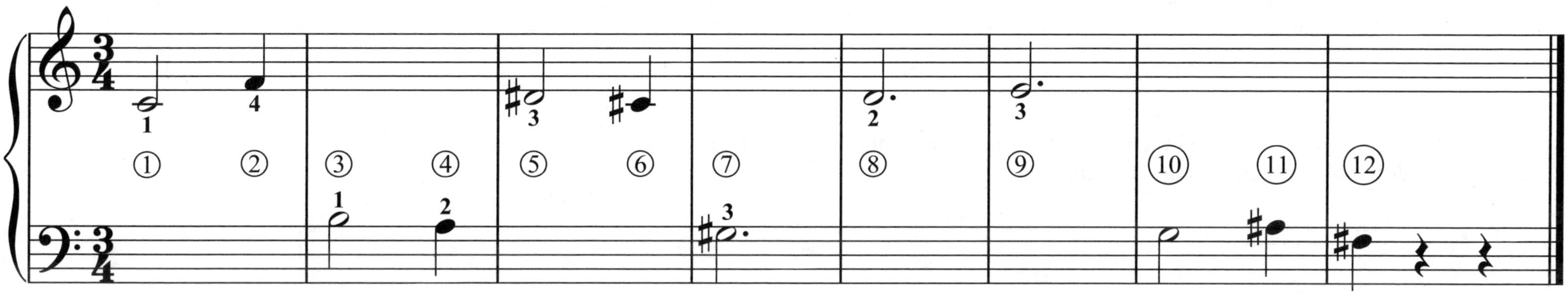

METER CHANGE

2. Now change the meter to $\frac{6}{8}$ and repeat some of the tones of the row before moving ahead. However, once you go to that next tone, do not go back in the row until you have played all of them.

These are just a few things that you can do with the series as you make up your own original twelve-tone pieces.

THE IV CHORD

So far you have used the I and V7 chords in major and minor. Now add the IV chord which is built on the fourth step of the scale.

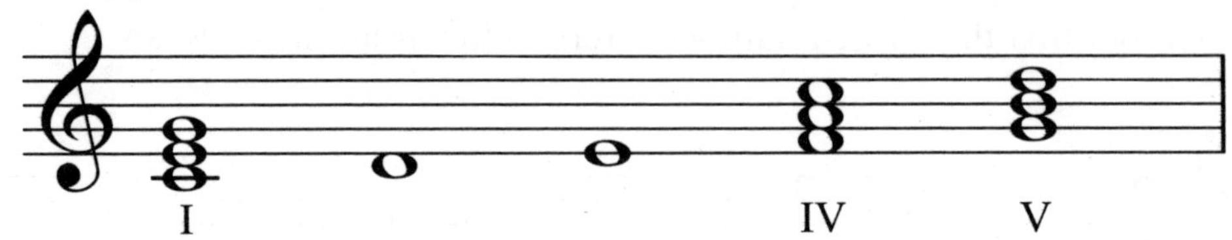

Notice as you go from the I to the IV chord that the top note of the I chord moves up *one whole step* while the middle note only moves up *one half step*.

FOR HE'S A JOLLY GOOD FELLOW

This song is harmonized with the I, IV, and V7 chords. In the last measure, *D. S. al Fine* tells you to go back to the sign (𝄋) and play to the word *Fine* (the end). Since this song has three sections (A B A), it is a *three part form*.

AUTUMN SONG

Play this song with block chords in the left hand, then play as written.

German Folk Melody

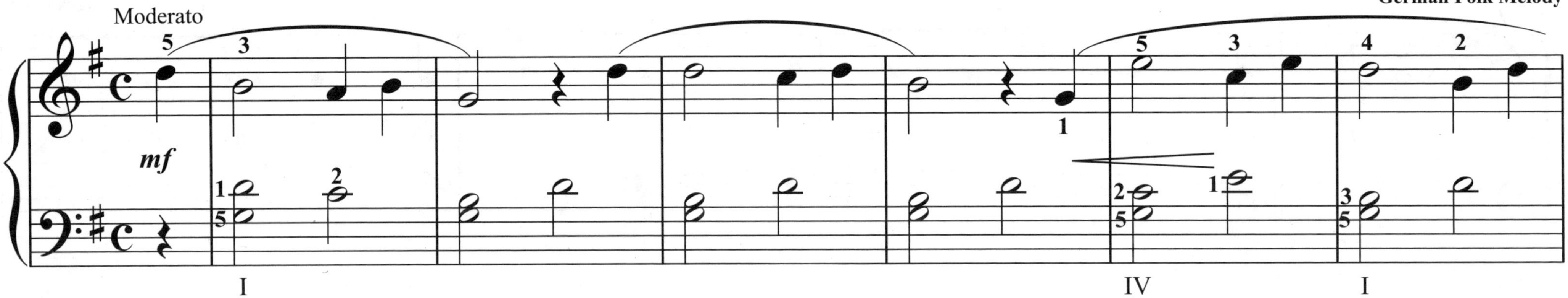

Also try it with an Alberti Bass

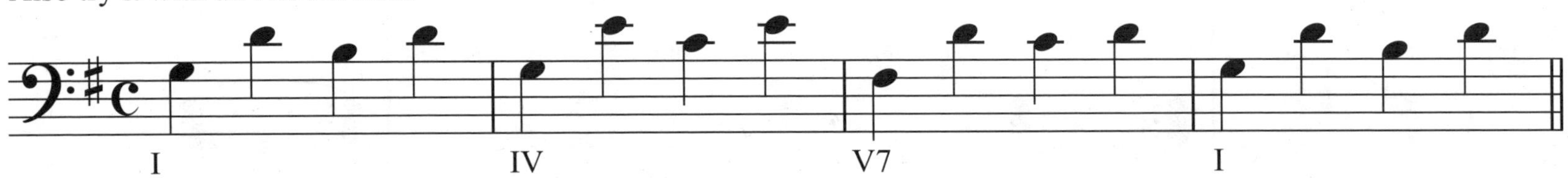

DANCE

Notice the repetitions, sequences and inversions in the melody. Play the left hand with a "down-up" wrist motion.

SEA SONG

1. Notice that this melody is harmonized with only the I and IV chords until the V7 chord in the last measure.
2. Check the melody for any repetitions and inversions.
3. Transpose this to F and G major.

DIMINISHED TRIADS

Major triads consist of a *major* third and a *perfect* fifth while minor triads have a *minor* third and a *perfect* fifth. Lower the fifth of a *minor* triad to make it *diminished*.

DIATONIC TRIADS

As you play a triad on each tone of the C Major scale, notice that the I, IV, and V chords are *major*, the ii, iii, and vi chords are *minor* and the seventh chord is *diminished*. It is the same for every major key.

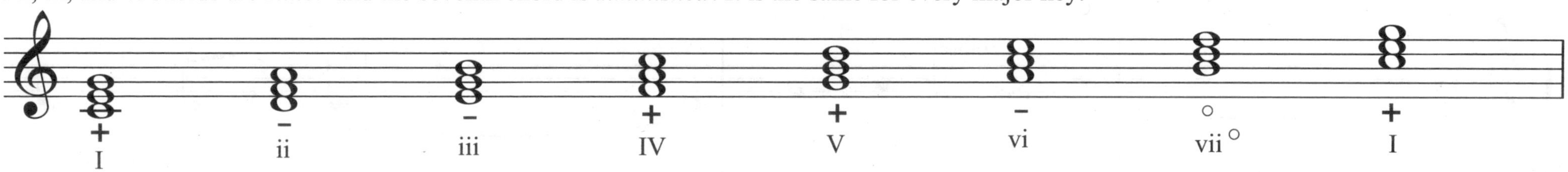

This melody is harmonized by triads moving up and down the C Major scale. After the first or second day, make up new melodies for these triads. You can use either 1/3/5 on every chord or the fingering shown here.

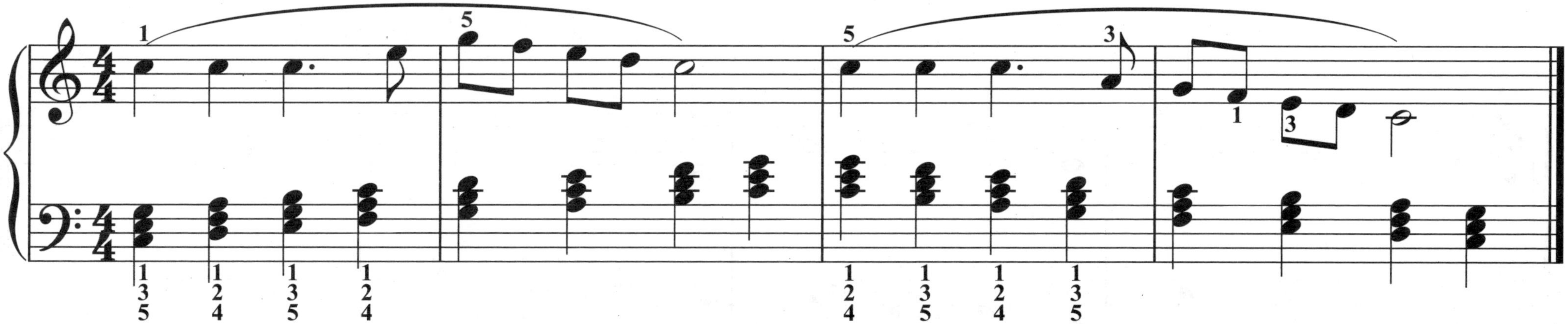

BOOGIE BLUES

First play as written, then create your own blues melodies for this bass pattern.

PARALLEL MOTION

There are two melodies here -- one for the right hand, and the other for the left hand. Play each part alone to get its sound, then put them together and notice how they both move in the same direction (called *parallel motion*.)

DUET

(Secondo)

After playing this as written, improvise new melodies in either Primo or Secondo.

DUET

(Primo)

QUIET TIME

Notice that the rhythm of each two measure phase is repeated until the last four measures.
Create other melodies with different rhytms. Also transpose this up one step to play it in the Phrygian mode.

MERRILY WE ROLL ALONG

Melodies can be harmonized by triads moving up or down the diatonic scale (see page 19). *Harmonic rhythm* is how often these chords are changed. Here the melody is harmonized by one chord per measure. Play as written, than change the *harmonic rhythm* and use two chords per measure.

Here are other "harmonic rhythms." Each day try a new one. (See pages 3 to 6, "Tricks with Triads," Book I)

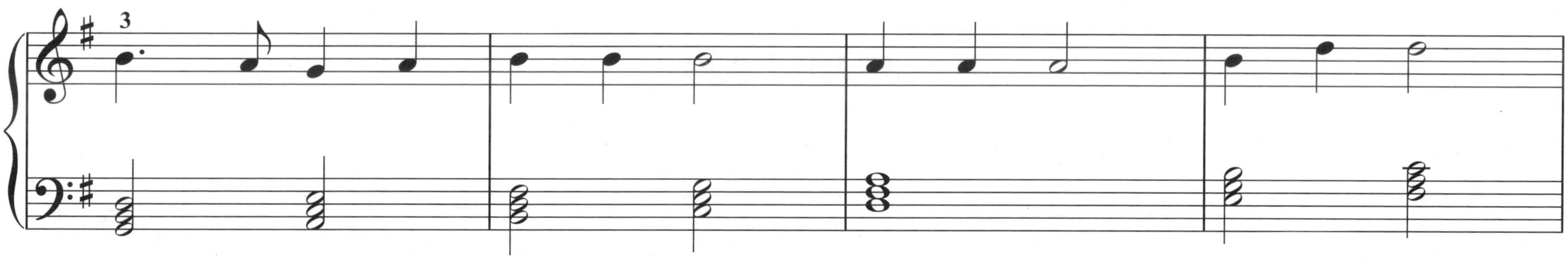

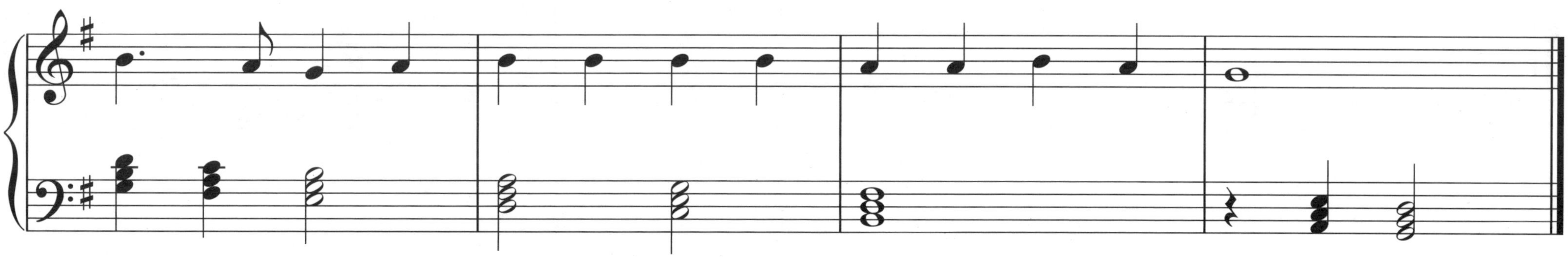

PRESTO

Think a slight crescendo in the first two measures of each phrase followed by a gradual diminuendo in the third and fourth measures. This will help avoid "bumping" repeated notes and will give a better phrase line.

Türk (adapted)

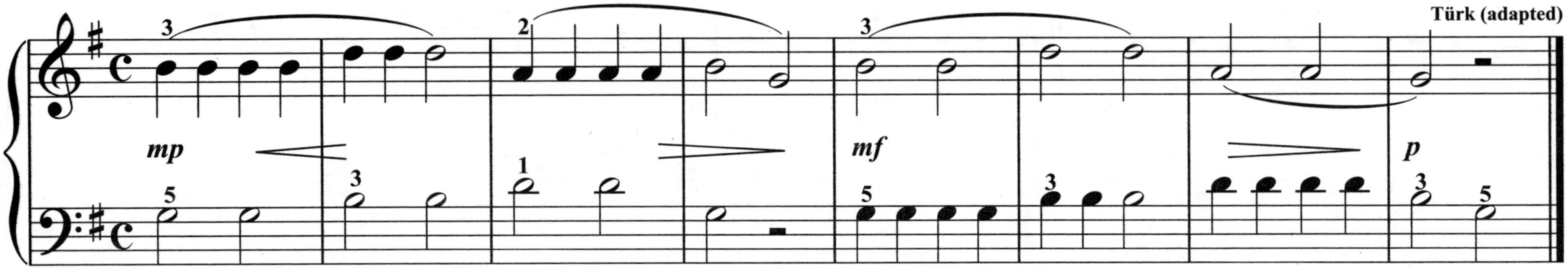

MODERATO

Play the left and right hands as if this were a duet. Tranpose to F, E and E♭ major.

Türk (adapted)

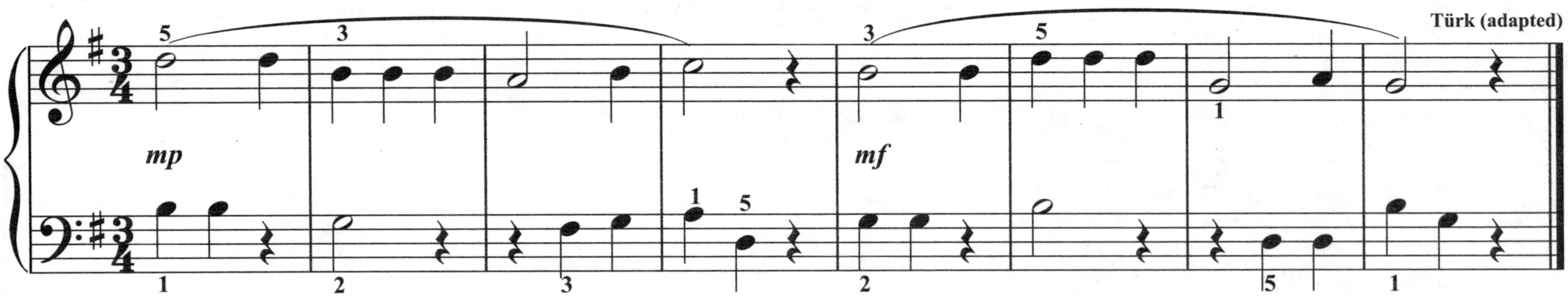

BLUE NOTES

The six different tones here make up the *Blues Scale*.

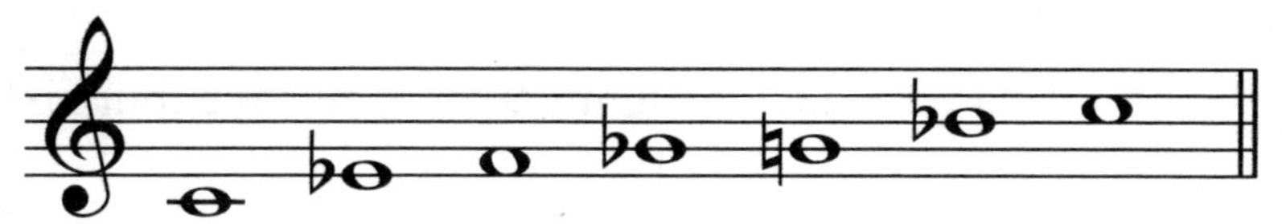

This blues melody is harmonized by a minor and major triad *ostinato*. After playing as written, create new blues melodies.

PENTATONIC TUNE

If you divide two eighth notes, you have four sixteenth notes:

To get the correct rhythm when you have a dotted eighth followed by a sixteenth note, think:
"do to‿do to‿do to‿do."

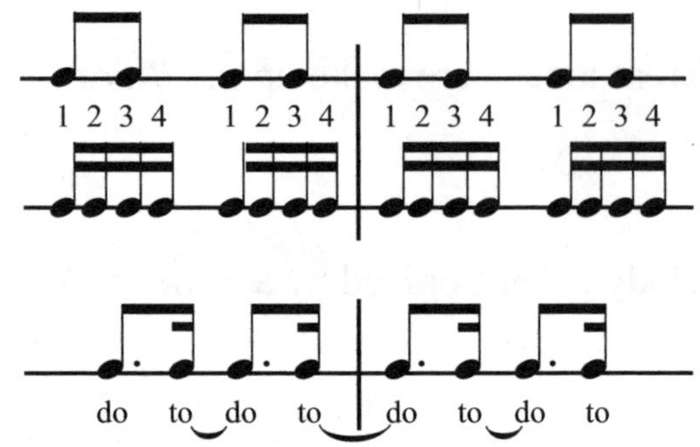

After playing this as written, make up new pentatonic melodies with the same rhythm.

MELODY HARMONIZATION IN MINOR

First play the i, iv, V7 and i chords in c minor, then play the song as written. Also transpose this to D and E minor.

CANON

In "Canon" one voice imitates the other exactly. First play the left hand, then the right hand to see that the melody is the same in both parts until the very end.

Transpose to D♭ and C Major.

PHRYGIAN DANCE

Since it is sometimes necessary to shift fingers from one key to another, watch your fingering carefully.
Transpose this to the Dorian mode (D to D on the white keys).

HAYO, HAYA

Since this melody has lots of skips, be sure to use the fingering as marked.

Chanukkah Song

ANDANTE

This fingering will help you get a smooth melody line. Also, make the left hand alberti bass accompaniment softer than the right hand melody. In the fourth bar we "borrow" the D Major chord as indicated by the accidental.

Roger Elston

HIGHLAND DANCE

(Secondo)

Observe the dynamics carefully and keep the melodic lines balanced between Primo and Secondo. Also, you can create new melodies for both parts.

HIGHLAND DANCE

(Primo)

Observe the dynamics carefully and keep the melodic lines balanced between Primo and Secondo.
Also, you can create new melodies for both parts.

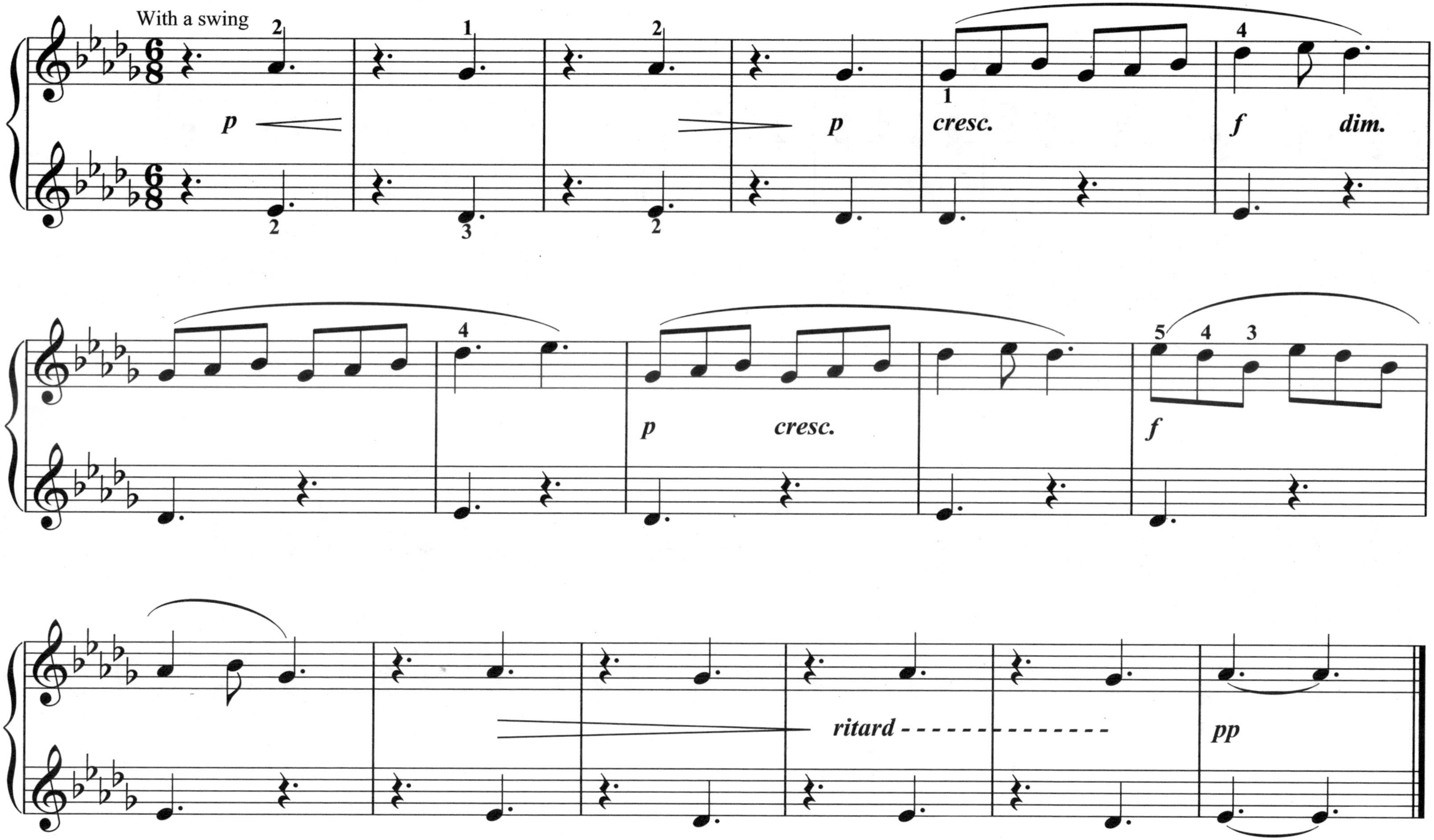

SURPRISE

You may use $\begin{smallmatrix}5\\3\\1\end{smallmatrix}$ in the right hand and $\begin{smallmatrix}1\\3\\5\end{smallmatrix}$ in the left hand on all triads or you may also use the 2nd and 4th fingers on some of them. Try both ways. Also, make the staccato notes half as long as those without staccato marks.

SAILOR BOY

In your mind, change this meter from $\frac{2}{4}$ to $\frac{4}{8}$.

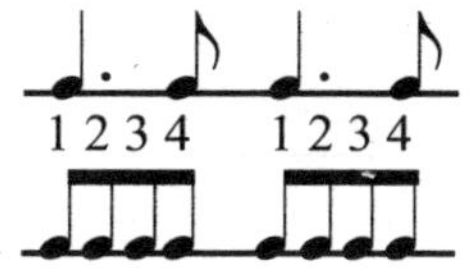

Also, think $\frac{8}{16}$ meter for the dotted eighth and sixteenth notes. Remember the dotted eighth note gets the same time as 3 sixteenth notes.

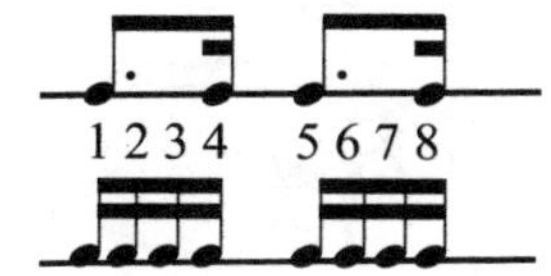

SCANDINAVIAN FOLK SONG

With spirit

ON YOUR TOES

This is a study of different intervals (2nds, 3rds, 4ths, etc.) Learn to identify them quickly as you sightread each new piece.

ETUDE

Notice that the 3rd finger passes *over* the thumb in the first phrase and the thumb passes *under* the 3rd finger in the second phrase.

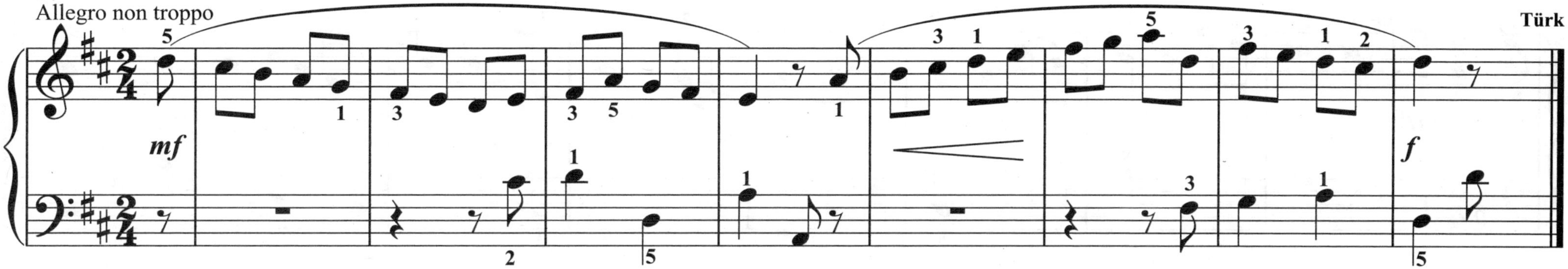

ETUDE

The left and right hand parts move in contrary motion except in measure seven, which is parallel motion.

MINUET

The triplet (♩♩♩ with a 3 over it) in the seventh measure gets the same amount of time as two eighths or one quarter.

OLD TALE

Play this very slowly and expressively and be sure to observe all dynamic markings. Use this same rhythm to create other melodies.

MARCH

Try different fingerings for the left hand chords to find the best for you.

MINUET

Mozart

THE CHASE

Use a slight wrist rotation on each five-note grouping and observe all dynamic markings carefully.

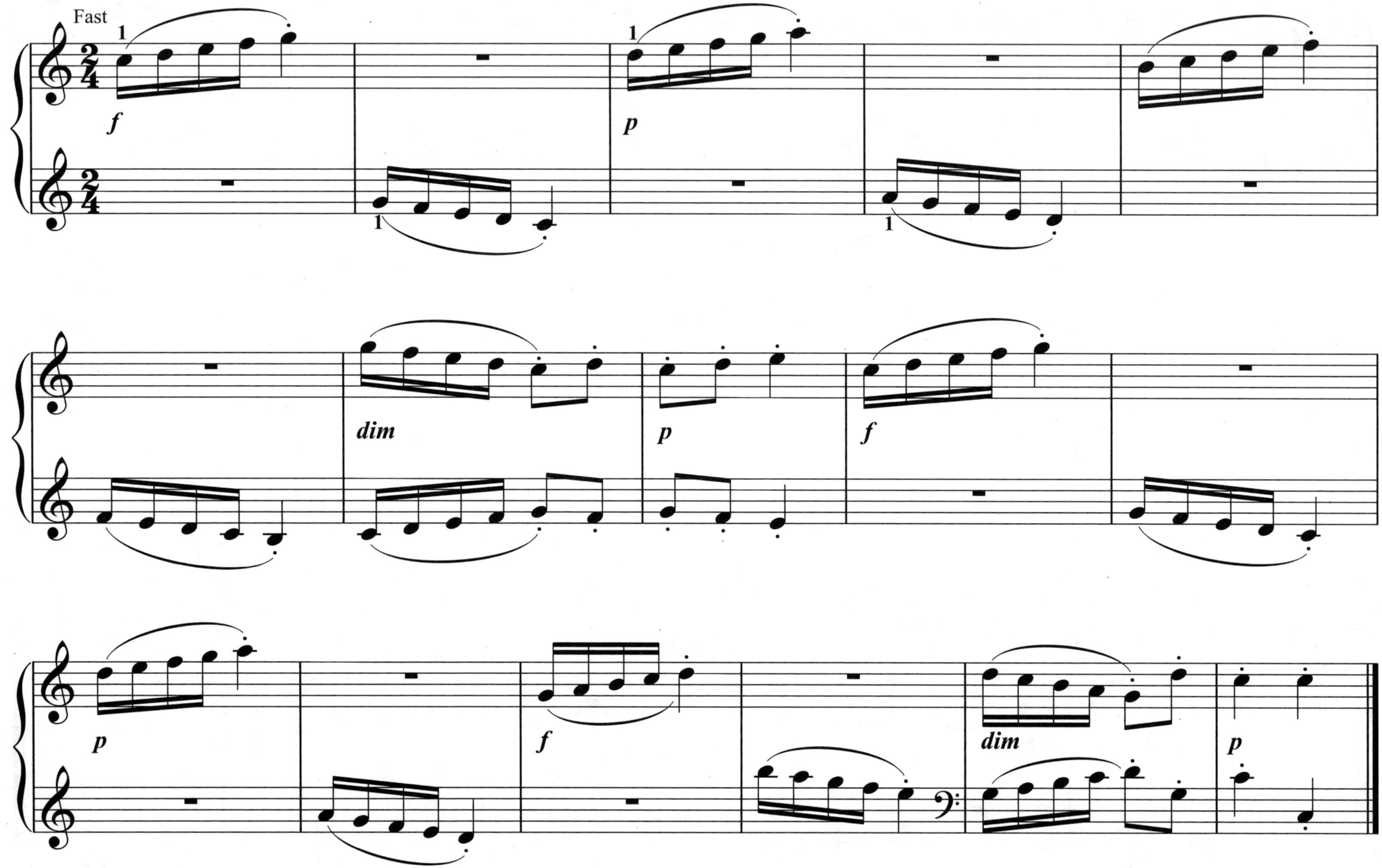

SAILOR'S DANCE

SOLDIER'S MARCH